THE SMARTEST ANIMALS

DOLPHINS

by Tammy Gagne

Content Consultant
Stan Kuczaj, PhD
Director, Marine Mammal Behavior and Cognition Lab
University of Southern Mississippi

CORE
LIBRARY

Published by ABDO Publishing Company, PO Box 398166, Minneapolis, MN 55439. Copyright © 2014 by Abdo Consulting Group, Inc. International copyrights reserved in all countries. No part of this book may be reproduced in any form without written permission from the publisher. The Core Library™ is a trademark and logo of ABDO Publishing Company.

Printed in the United States of America,
North Mankato, Minnesota
092013
012014

♻ THIS BOOK CONTAINS AT LEAST 10% RECYCLED MATERIALS.

Editor: Mirella Miller
Series Designer: Becky Daum

Library of Congress Cataloging-in-Publication Data
Gagne, Tammy.
  Dolphins / by Tammy Gagne.
      pages cm. -- (The smartest animals)
  Includes bibliographical references and index.
  ISBN 978-1-62403-166-3
  1. Dolphins--Juvenile literature. I. Title.
  QL737.C432.G34 2014
  599.53'4--dc23
                        2013027401

Photo Credits: Melissa Schalke/Shutterstock Images, cover, 1; iStockphoto/Thinkstock, 4, 12, 34; Dominic Laniewicz/Shutterstock Images, 7; Potapov Alexander/Shutterstock Images/Red Line Editorial, 9; Tom Middleton/Shutterstock Images, 10; Sea Life Park Hawaii/PRNewsFoto/AP Images, 15, 43; Fuse/Thinkstock, 16, 36; Palis Michalis/Shutterstock Images, 18, 45; Kike Calvo/AP Images, 20; Minden Pictures/SuperStock, 23; Janet Mann/National Academy of Sciences/AP Images, 25; Biosphoto/SuperStock, 26; Morales/Age Fotostock/SuperStock, 28; Red Line Editorial, 30; Science and Society/SuperStock, 32; Willyam Bradberry/Shutterstock Images, 39; Top Photo Group/Thinkstock, 40

CONTENTS

A HERO WITH FLIPPERS

Fourteen-year-old Davide Ceci was on a small boat with his father in the Adriatic Sea in 2000. Davide was hanging on the boat ladder and fell off and into the water. The teenager could not swim, and his father had not seen him fall. Luckily for Davide, a skilled swimmer was in the same waters off the coast of Manfredonia in Italy. Filippo was not just any helpful stranger, though. He was a dolphin.

Dolphins swim in Earth's oceans and rivers. These super-smart animals interact, play, and communicate with each other and humans.

Filippo quickly swam underneath Davide and pushed him up to the water's surface as the boy gulped for air. Davide grabbed hold of Filippo when he realized what was pushing him. Filippo carried Davide back to his father's boat.

Davide's mother calls Filippo a hero for having "the instinct to save a human life." Dolphins are smart animals. Filippo is one of many dolphins that have shown intelligent behaviors.

Dolphin Senses

Dolphins have sharp senses. Their vision works well above water and underwater. Dolphins can also hear better than most humans. They can detect sounds people cannot. Dolphins are sensitive to touch. They use this sense for bonding with other dolphins. Little is known about dolphins' sense of taste, but their sense of smell is not highly developed.

Dolphin Basics

Some people think dolphins are a type of fish because they live in water. But dolphins are actually mammals. Fish breathe through gills, but dolphins breathe through lungs. Dolphins must swim to the water's surface to breathe.

Dolphins must come to the water's surface often to breathe.

Like other mammals, dolphins are warm-blooded and give birth to live babies.

More than 30 kinds of dolphins have been discovered around the world. The most common is the bottlenose dolphin. Bottlenose dolphins are seen on television shows and can be found at aquariums. Other common dolphins include the spinner dolphin

An Old Discovery

In February of 2012, Noah Cook and his mother made an unbelievable discovery. While walking along a Maryland beach, they discovered the top of what is believed to be a 12-million-year-old dolphin skull. Paleontologists have labeled fossils from as many as 30 different kinds of whales and dolphins in the nearby area known as Calvert Cliffs. A find this old is rare. Belonging to the extinct *Lophocetus pappus* species, the remains were the third specimen of the species ever found.

and orcas. Although orcas are commonly called killer whales, they belong to the dolphin family.

Dolphin Features

The first thing most people notice about a dolphin is its rostrum. A rostrum is a long snout that looks like a nose. The rostrum is not used for breathing though. Dolphins have a blowhole on the top of their heads for breathing. They use their rostrums for picking up and tossing objects when playing. They also use their rostrums for digging fish from the sea floor.

A dolphin's large, round forehead makes it easy to recognize. It is called the melon. Dolphins have

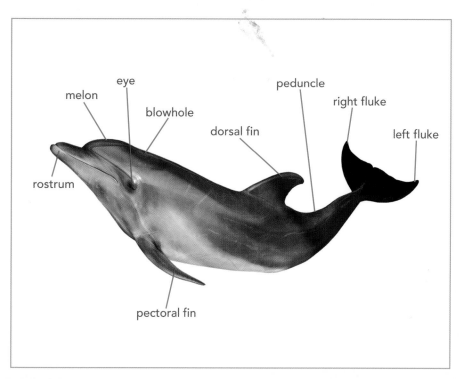

Dolphin Features

Each of a dolphin's body parts serves a special purpose. This diagram shows where these parts are located on a dolphin. How might some of these parts help a dolphin hunt for food? Or breathe?

smooth black, white, or gray skin that feels like rubber.

Dolphins have five fins. The fins on a dolphin's two sides are called pectoral fins. The single fin on a dolphin's back is its dorsal fin. A dolphin's tail is called the peduncle. The peduncle is divided into a right fluke and a left fluke.

Orcas are the heaviest and largest dolphin species.

Most bottlenose dolphins are between 6.6 feet and 12.8 feet (2 m and 3.9 m) long. They weigh between 330 pounds and 440 pounds (150 kg and 200 kg). The size of other types of dolphins varies greatly. Some dolphins weigh as little as 90 pounds (40 kg) and are 4 feet (1.2 m) long. Other dolphins, such as the orca, weigh up to 11 short tons (10 metric tons) and are nearly 30 feet (9 m) long.

FURTHER EVIDENCE

Chapter One covers basic information about dolphins. What is the main point of the chapter? What key evidence supports this point? Check out the Web site below. Find a quote from the Web site that supports the chapter's main point. Does the quote support the evidence presented in the chapter or add new evidence?

Dolphin Facts
www.mycorelibrary.com/dolphins

CHAPTER TWO

A VERY SOCIAL LIFE

Dolphins are social animals. A group of dolphins is called a school or a pod. A pod has between 2 and 30 dolphins. Several pods can join together to form a super pod of hundreds to thousands of dolphins. Being part of a pod is important for dolphins' survival. Hunting together means each pod member has enough to eat. Dolphins also work together to protect the pod from predators.

Dolphin pods range in size. All pod members work together to survive.

Mating

Female dolphins start mating between the ages of 5 and 14. Females mature faster than males. They look for the strongest, most dominant males to be their partners. Then their babies are more likely to be strong and healthy. Males often fight for a female's attention. A male may make forceful sounds as a warning to another male. He might even bump into another male to get him to back down.

Auntie Dolphins

A dolphin dad does not help care for his young, but another member of the pod often does. Known as the auntie dolphin, this pod member stays close to a new mother and her calf following birth. The auntie dolphin is not always female. Males can also help.

Female dolphins are pregnant for approximately 12 months. They will not become pregnant again for two or three years after giving birth. Female dolphins mate with multiple males throughout their lifetimes. They give birth to one baby at a time. Dolphin

Dolphin calves stay close to their mothers during the first years of their lives.

babies are called calves. Newborn calves usually measure between two feet and eight feet (55 cm and 2.4 m) long, depending on the species. They weigh between 10 pounds (4.5 kg) and 350 pounds (160 kg). Calves are darker in color than adult dolphins. They also have light-colored vertical lines down their sides. These lines disappear in the first year of a calf's life.

Growing Up

Mother dolphins stay close to their babies. A calf depends on its mother's slipstream to help it swim.

Male dolphins create strong bonds with other males throughout their lives.

The slipstream is a water current created by the mother as she moves through the water. Calves stay with their mothers for up to six years. Fathers sometimes live in the same pod as the mothers and calves. However, they do not help raise the young.

Dolphins leave their pods as adults. They come back to visit their home pods throughout their lifetimes. Males may join several different pods during their lifetimes. Young males form strong bonds with males from other pods. These males can remain together for decades.

Hunting and Sleeping

Dolphins are active during the day and at night. They are usually busiest in the early morning and in the evening when they are hunting for food. Dolphins use their sharp hearing to help them find food. Most dolphins eat fish, squid, and crabs. Some larger dolphins prey on other mammals.

Dolphins can stay awake for up to two weeks at a time. They rest part of their brain while the other part stays active. Being partly alert allows dolphins to spot sharks and other predators

And the Record Holder Is. . .

In 2013, at 63 years old, a female bottlenose dolphin called Nicklo was the oldest known bottlenose dolphin in the world. She and her 60-year-old female pod member, known as BlackTipDoubleDip, are often seen swimming together in Florida's Sarasota Bay. Nicklo's daughter and grandcalf have also been spotted in these waters.

Dolphins that live at zoos and aquariums tend to live longer than dolphins in the wild.

before they attack. It also helps dolphins breathe regularly. Dolphins must return to the water's surface every 6 to 20 minutes for air.

The lifespan of a dolphin depends on the dolphin species. Bottlenose dolphins live at least 20 years. A small number of dolphins have been known to live as long as 50 years. Captive dolphins tend to live longer than dolphins in the wild. This is likely because wild dolphins face many more risks such as predators, habitat loss, and pollution.

Dr. Kathleen M. Dudzinski and Dr. Toni Frohoff are scientists who study dolphins. In their book, *Dolphin Mysteries: Unlocking the Secrets of Communication*, they describe discoveries made about bottlenose dolphins in Shark Bay in western Australia:

> *Over the years, [dolphin] researchers have made a variety of startling discoveries that suggest an extremely complicated social structure. One discovery is the concept of the male alliance: two or three males who form a long-term alliance, cooperating to herd females during mating periods. Some male alliances are so close that the dolphins spend nearly every waking second in each other's company; alliances can continue for up to twenty years. . . . They have very strong preferences about whom they will associate with.*

Source: Kathleen Dudzinski and Toni Frohoff. Dolphin Mysteries: Unlocking the Secrets of Communication. *New Haven, CT: Yale University Press, 2008. Print. 107.*

What's the Big Idea?

Take a close look at Dr. Dudzinski and Dr. Frohoff's discoveries. What is their main idea? What evidence is used to support their points? Come up with a few sentences showing how Dr. Dudzinski and Dr. Frohoff use two or three pieces of evidence to support their main point.

CHAPTER THREE

TALES OF INTELLIGENCE

Scientists rank dolphins among the most intelligent animals in the world. An adult bottlenose dolphin's brain weighs three and a half pounds (1.6 kg). That is 25 percent heavier than the brain of a human. However, it is dolphin behavior that has made so many people want to study this special animal.

Dolphins are known for communicating with, playing with, and protecting other dolphins in their pod.

Most dolphins spend their time with other dolphins. They communicate with one another. They also love to play with pod members and humans.

Sonar Abilities

Dolphins depend on their sonar ability to understand the world around them. Sonar uses sound waves that are bounced off of objects. Dolphins do not just hear sounds. They also send out fast clicks through their melons. The sound waves from these clicks bounce off an object and return to the dolphin. Dolphins receive the sounds through their jaws. These sounds are then sent to the dolphin's middle ear and brain. The brain turns the sounds into

Working with the US Navy

Dolphins are capable of finding a variety of objects, both near and far. These include underwater mines. The US Navy has been training bottlenose dolphins to help its sailors locate explosives since the 1960s. The dolphins do not get close to the mines, since their sonar abilities sense the mine from a distance. Once a dolphin locates a mine, navy sailors can dismantle it or avoid it.

A dolphin uses its melon for sonar.

three-dimensional images. Sonar also helps dolphins know when predators are approaching. They can use it to detect the size, shape, and speed of objects as far as one quarter of a mile (0.4 km) away.

Dolphins also use sonar for understanding objects. When they find a new item, they sweep their heads back and forth. This usually means they are using sonar. Biologist Julia Whitty and filmmaker Hardy Jones spent 20 years studying spotted dolphins in the Bahamas. Jones observed dolphins using sonar when he dropped his swim fin in the water. The dolphins circled around the fin moving their heads back and forth.

Communication Skills

Dolphins are good at communicating with one another through sounds. Some of the frequencies at which they make noises are very high. Humans can only hear these sounds by recording them and playing them back at much slower speeds.

Playful and Protective

Scientists know dolphins play with objects for fun. They might play with seaweed and coral by using them to make bubbles underwater. More recently, researchers have observed dolphins using objects for

Creating and using tools, such as sea sponges, are smart behaviors scientists have seen dolphins practicing.

more than just fun. Sometimes they turn objects into tools. Bottlenose dolphins in Australia, for example, sometimes break off sponges from the sea floor. Afterward they keep the sponges on their rostrums as they poke the sand in search of food. The sponges protect the dolphins' rostrums.

A pod will protect a pregnant dolphin that is ready to give birth.

Scientists have also seen dolphins be serious. One day a group of dolphins was seen gathering in a tight formation. The scientists studying the dolphins thought a predator was approaching. When none appeared, the scientists took a closer look. The pod was gathering around a pregnant female. They were protecting her as she was preparing to give birth.

Diana Reiss is the director of the Dolphin Research Program in Baltimore, Maryland. One of her experiments involved placing a mirror in a pool with two dolphins, Delphi and Pan. She wanted to see if the dolphins would recognize their reflections:

> Dolphins are curious creatures, always ready to investigate. . . their environment. So it wasn't surprising that when we lifted the tarp from the mirror, Delphi and Pan were eager to check it out. . . . They touched its surface with their beaks and aimed a lot of [sonar] signals at it. It must have been very odd for them to see what appeared to be three-dimensional objects in front of them. . . while getting a sonar signal of an essentially flat surface. . . . They quickly began to interact with the reflections in the mirror as if they were other dolphins. . . . they circled and cocked their heads, rocked their bodies back and forth, and opened and closed their mouths.

Source: Diana Reiss. The Dolphin in the Mirror: Exploring Dolphin Minds and Saving Dolphin Lives. New York: Houghton Mifflin, 2011. Print. 143.

Consider Your Audience

Read the passage above closely. How could you adapt Reiss's words for a different audience, such as your parents or younger friends? Write a blog post conveying this same information for the new audience. What is the best way to get your point across?

CHAPTER FOUR

AT HOME THROUGHOUT THE WORLD

Dolphins are found in every ocean on Earth. They even live in some rivers. The Amazon River dolphin lives in South America. These dolphins are known for their pink skin, which can also have brown or light gray areas. Bottlenose dolphins live in every ocean except for the Arctic Ocean and the Antarctic Ocean. Spotted dolphins live in the Atlantic

The Amazon River dolphin lives in the Amazon River of South America.

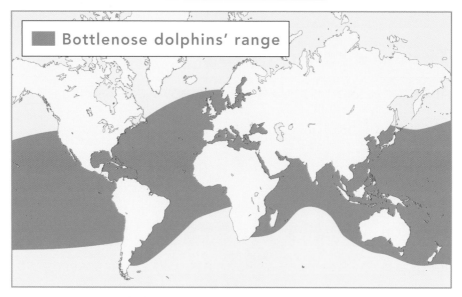

Bottlenose Dolphins' Range

Look at the range map of all the different locations that bottlenose dolphins call home. Why would bottlenose dolphins be well suited for these habitats? Write a short paragraph describing a bottlenose dolphin's habitat.

and Pacific oceans. They avoid the Arctic Ocean and the Antarctic Ocean.

Most dolphins live in deep, saltwater environments. A few dolphin species live in freshwater areas. The majority of dolphins prefer warmer temperatures, but they will move into cooler areas when necessary. Dolphins often travel to new areas in search of food.

Threats to Dolphins

Another reason dolphins might leave an area is because of habitat loss. As humans spend more time on and near the water, dolphins are losing their homes. Boating and other marine activities cause pollution. This affects dolphins' skin. Their skin is sensitive to chemicals that boats and other watercraft leave behind.

Humans also pose a threat to dolphins through fishing. Dolphins live in many of the same areas as tuna. Tuna is a popular fish humans catch to eat or sell to markets. Dolphins often get caught in nets put out for the tuna. Baby dolphins face an especially high risk since they are smaller. When fishers reach the dolphins to untangle them, the animals are often injured or have already died.

Tuna Companies

Starting in the late 1950s, many fishers intentionally chased and set nets on dolphins. Dolphins were easier to spot than tuna. These fishers set their nets

CES

UNKS

E

185g

GUARA

This produc
selected an
and should
condition. I

DOLPHIN FRIENDLY

By 1994 all major tuna companies in the United States had added a dolphin-safe phrase to their labels.

on dolphins knowing tuna swam below. Animal rights groups helped create awareness of this practice during the 1980s and the 1990s. Their campaigns helped make sure tuna companies would not cast nets near dolphins. Major tuna companies added dolphin-safe labels to their cans. This meant the tuna was caught in an area without trying to catch dolphins too.

Natural Threats

In addition to human threats, dolphins also face natural predators, such as large sharks. A shark may attack a dolphin if it is separated from its pod. Sharks will not attack a group of dolphins. If one dolphin is threatened, other pod members will protect it. Working together, a dolphin pod could kill a shark.

Many types of dolphins are on the endangered species list. This means they are at risk of becoming extinct. The endangered dolphins include the Ganges River dolphin, the Hector's dolphin, the Irrawaddy dolphin, the Amazon River dolphin, and the

An Ongoing Problem

In 1994 the United States stopped importing tuna from parts of the world where fishers targeted dolphins in their fishing practices. Still, thousands of dolphins in the Eastern tropical Pacific Ocean die each year due to tuna fishing.

Boat pollution in Earth's oceans and rivers is putting dolphins in danger.

Indus River dolphin. The decline in numbers among these dolphins is mostly due to human activity. New technology makes the problem worse with bigger boats and increased pollution.

Interacting with Dolphins

Many scientists work hard to teach people about dolphins and the threats facing them. The scientists hope as people learn more about dolphins, they will work harder to protect them. Many aquariums offer people the chance to interact with dolphins. Some even allow visitors to swim with these amazing creatures. If you encounter a dolphin in person, it is important to remember some basic rules. Touching a dolphin can scare the animal. Do not touch it unless it comes to you. Never chase a dolphin. Listen underwater. It is easier to hear dolphin sounds below water. Always listen to the guide and follow his or her instructions.

On the Rise

One of the rarest dolphins is the Chinese white dolphin. But despite concerns over pollution in its native waters, the population of this species is growing. In 2004 there were only 98 Chinese white dolphins in the Qinzhou Port's Sanniang Bay area. By 2012 the total had increased to 140.

CHAPTER FIVE

LEARNING MORE

Dolphins are smart. But experts argue whether these animals understand emotions in the same way people do. Scientists study dolphins and other mammals to see if they can feel emotions. Dolphins and other mammals have a limbic system in their brains. This system helps an animal experience feelings such as happiness, anger, and fear. Although dolphins can feel emotions, scientists question

Scientists still have much to learn about dolphins and their intelligence.

whether they understand the feelings. Researchers are still working on the answer to this mystery.

Talking with Dolphins

After observing spotted dolphins in the Bahamas for a while, a group of scientists decided to try communicating with them. They recorded sounds made by the dolphins. Then they played the sounds underwater using special computers. The researchers were surprised when the dolphins responded by copying the humans. The dolphins moved their bodies into upright positions as if they were standing. Other dolphins lay on the ocean

A Different Kind of Trick

Professor Stan Kuczaj discovered that dolphins are smart enough to be tricky. He taught a group of dolphins to pick up items tossed into their tank. For each item a dolphin picked up, he would give it a fish as a reward. He quickly noticed a female dolphin named Kelly was picking up items thrown in the water mistakenly by tourists. Kelly hid them under a drain cover. When other dolphins were not around, Kelly would bring out these secret items to try and get a reward.

It is important for dolphin researchers to spend as much time as possible with dolphins in order to better understand their behavior and intelligence.

floor like members of the scuba-diving research team were doing. The dolphins also repeated the sounds scientists played from the computer.

The computer allowed scientists to communicate on a very limited basis with the dolphins. It took two decades for technology to allow for this limited communication. Scientists hope to use advancing technology to take their work with dolphins further.

Humans must keep Earth's oceans and rivers clean to protect dolphins and other marine life.

They plan to use a computer to study the noises dolphins make in different situations.

Researcher Ken Norris studied the recordings of noises made by recently captured dolphins. He and other scientists believe dolphins do more than call out names when they become separated. The animals also make sounds that express their feelings.

Scientists are hopeful the future holds even more fascinating dolphin discoveries. Some dolphin species are endangered and are threatened by certain human activities. It is important for humans to help take care of the oceans and rivers dolphins live in. Taking care of the oceans and rivers means scientists will continue to make amazing discoveries about dolphins.

EXPLORE ONLINE

The focus of Chapter Five is on scientific research on dolphins. The Web site below focuses on dolphins' language and communication. As you know, every source is different. How is the information given on the Web site different from the information in this chapter? What details are the same? How do the two sources present facts differently? What can you learn from this Web site?

Dolphin Language
www.mycorelibrary.com/dolphins

Common Name: Dolphin

Scientific Name: *Delphinidae* or *Platanistidae*

Average Size: From 4 feet (1.2 m) to 30 feet (9 m) long; the bottlenose dolphin averages 8 feet (2.4 m) long

Average Weight: From 90 pounds (40 kg) to 11 short tons (10 metric tons); the bottlenose dolphin averages between 440 pounds (200 kg) and 660 pounds (300 kg)

Color: Black, white, or gray

Lifespan: 20 to 70 years

Diet: Variety of fish, squid, crab, mammals

Habitat: Worldwide in oceans and rivers

Threats: Sharks and humans

Intelligence Features

- Dolphins can stay awake for up to two weeks by resting only part of their brains.
- Dolphins use sonar to detect the size, shape, and speed of objects both near and far away.
- Dolphins use objects in their environment as tools.

STOP AND THINK

Say What?

Learning about dolphins can mean learning a lot of new vocabulary. Find five words in this book that you've never heard or seen before. Use a dictionary to find out what they mean. Using your own ideas, write down the meaning of each word. Then use each word in a new sentence.

Another View

There are many different sources about dolphins. As you know, every source is different. Ask a librarian or another adult to help you find a reliable source about dolphins. Write a short essay comparing and contrasting the new source's point of view with the ideas in this book. How are the sources similar? How are the sources different? Why do you think they are similar or different?

Take a Stand

This book discusses some of the problems that occur when humans fish for tuna in the same places that dolphins live. Take a position on tuna fishing in dolphins' home range. Then write a short essay explaining your opinion. Make sure you give reasons for your opinion. Give some evidence to support those reasons.

Tell the Tale

Chapter Two discusses characteristics and behaviors of dolphins. Write 200 words about a dolphin community. Be sure to set the scene, develop a sequence of events, and offer a conclusion.

GLOSSARY

captive
kept within bounds

current
water moving in a certain
direction

dominant
controlling over others

endangered species
a species threatened with
extinction

instinct
a natural ability

paleontologist
a person who studies fossil
remains

sonar
a method for detecting
objects underwater by sound

species
groups of living things that
can breed with each other

specimen
a small amount of something
that represents an entire
group

three-dimensional
having or seeming to have
depth

warm-blooded
animals whose body
temperature remains the
same, whatever their
surroundings

LEARN MORE

Books

Gunderson, Megan M. *Freshwater Dolphins*. Minneapolis: ABDO, 2011.

Haney, Johannah. *Endangered! Dolphins*. Tarrytown, NY: Marshall Cavendish, 2011.

Simon, Seymour. *Dolphins*. New York: HarperCollins, 2011.

Web Links

To learn more about dolphins, visit ABDO Publishing Company online at **www.abdopublishing.com**. Web sites about dolphins are featured on our Book Links page. These links are routinely monitored and updated to provide the most current information available.

Visit **www.mycorelibrary.com** for free additional tools for teachers and students.

INDEX

ABOUT THE AUTHOR

Tammy Gagne has written dozens of books for both adults and children. She resides in northern New England with her husband, son, and pets. One of her favorite pastimes is visiting schools to speak to students about the writing process.